SELLING TECHNIQUES MADE EASY!

*(The secret ingredients of success
are within your reach.)*

Jeffery T. Quinn

ISBN 978-1-105-92255-8

TABLE OF CONTENTS

PREFACE

Shut Up and Write!

I've been selling face-to-face (and over the phone, through the mail, more recently online) for more than twenty-five years. And one thing that I'm good at is *talking*.

Okay, maybe I'm *necessarily* good at it. But I do love it. Maybe that's why I went into sales to begin with.

For a lot of those years, I haven't just talked when selling …I've talked *about* selling, to pretty much anyone who will listen. New salespeople. Veterans like me. My family. My friends. The dog.

The thing is, I love selling – the actual *process*. What works? What doesn't? And of course the stories that old pro's and newbies have about their companies, their clients, their products and why they love it, too. Or hate it. Or often both at the same time.

It was my daughter who finally got tired of it. "Dad," she said, "I've heard all these stories a thousand times. Your friends have heard them, too. Even the *dog* is getting tired of it. If you have so much to say about this, why don't you just shut up and *write?*"

I have to admit, it pulled me up short. I had never actually thought about writing this stuff down, talking about it on paper. The fact is, I'm not much of a typist or even a reader.

"That doesn't matter," my daughter told me. "They have things called "recording devices" now, you know. In fact, there's one on that phone you love so much.

So we made a deal: I would make a few notes (I'm good at notes), talk into a little digital recorder, and she would write transcribe it. And maybe – just maybe – we'd end up with a book.

And look what happened.

This book is the culmination of almost a quarter century of experience in sales – and not just mine. It took almost a year to put this together, and over that time I started talking to other salespeople and clients about the project, and heard even more stories, got even more advice and tips – some of which I even agreed with. You'll find those in here, too; I even give credit where credit is due. Sometimes.

I think it's worthwhile for anyone who is into sales already or even considering it. The idea was to start more conversations, spark some new thoughts, trigger a few experiments, and ultimately make you better at your job.

I don't expect everyone to love sales as much as I do. But I *do* expect everyone to get something out of what they find here. If you do – or if you don't! – drop me an email at jtqhhi@yahoo.com and tell me what you think. Who knows, it might start yet another conversation … and you know how much I love to talk.

Okay, shut up and read!

CHAPTER ONE

It's not that hard ...
and it's not that easy

I've looked across the desk maybe a thousand new (or at least potential) salespeople – old and young, male and female, over-educated and fresh out of high school. And generally they fall into two categories.

As the newbie looks at me, all bright-eyed and ready to get rich, they are thinking one of two things:

- **This is gonna be easy.** All I have to do is smile big and be charming, and money will fall into my lap.
- **This is gonna be too hard.** I'm just not suited to sales. I don't like to ask people for money. But maybe this is better than [fill in the blank: working at McDonald's, staying home with the kids, moving to Alaska to work on the pipeline.]

The fact is ... they're both wrong and they're both right.

Being a successful salesperson isn't just a matter of (to paraphrase Arthur Miller) having a good smile and shined shoes – especially in the twenty-first century, when competition is more fierce than ever, and when it's way too easy for people to be their own (incompetent) salespeople. It requires some study, some creative thought, and keeping your brain engaged at all times. It's *work* … but like all good work, it's something you can actually come to love.

On the other hand, you'd be amazed at the range of people who are really good at sales. Bottom line: *there are no entry requirements,* beyond desire and a willingness to try.

- You don't need to have experience (though you probably do – you just don't know it)
- You don't need to be young (though you need to have energy)
- You don't need to be the smartest person you ever met (but you do need to have focus)
- You don't need to be a man
- You don't need to be a woman

- You don't need to have start-up money (though eating on a regular basis and having a roof over your head – those are *good* things)

- You don't need to know about sales already

I've known people at every level of experience, from every walk of life, beginning at every age, and even with significant health and mobility issues become truly *excellent* sales people, making anything from decent to *incredible* money. The most common obstacles – the ones you'd assume, the ones listed above – really don't apply.

But here are the things you *do* need:

- You need to want to be successful
- You need to be ready to work
- You need to *pay attention to people*
- You need to be honest – with yourself, with the people you work with, with the people you're trying to sell to
- You need to be resilient, persistent, and determined

If you have trouble with any of those things – particularly that one in the middle the one about *honesty* – then you'd better rethink your career choice.

Otherwise ... welcome to the club! I think you'll find a lot of worthwhile information – maybe even some insight – in this book.

So enough with the handshakes, smiles, and shined shoes.

Let's get to it!

A Word on Honesty

Here's the single most common misconception about salespeople:

*They're **all a bunch of crooks and liars. They'll say anything to make a sale and gouge as much money out of you as they can. That's just the way they ARE.***

Not one word of that is true. *Good* salespeople – the ones that last for more than one job or more than a few months – can't do *any* of that and stay employed or make any money. Because there's a basic difference between a *salesperson* and a *con artist*. *Everybody* – including me – has been swindled by a con artist at one time or another. Whether it's a crooked door-to-door 'salesman', or a flimflammer on the phone, or some short-term dude or babe at the used car lot preying on the innocent and trusting, it's happened. Admit it.

But these aren't salespeople. Salespeople *have* to be honest, because they want to sell to their customers *more than once*. They want customers for a *lifetime,* not for a single shot. And if they're not straight with those customers, if they try to overcharge or overpromise, they're shooting themselves in the foot – or maybe even a little higher up (think about it). So if you're looking for advice on how to be a con artist, look elsewhere. Go watch reruns of *The Rockford Files* or rent *The Sting*. You won't find it here. If you want to learn how to become the best salesperson you can be, using all your natural abilities, your common sense, and some 'tricks of the trade' … read on.

CHAPTER TWO

Know Yourself

I know this is going to sound kind of 'touchy-feely' for a book on salesmanship ... but trust me, you need to do this.

We talked about *honesty* a minute ago, and that extends – actually, it *starts* – with you being honest with and about *yourself*.

Everybody has strengths. Everybody has weaknesses. Everybody has talents and everybody has things that they can't do well, no matter how hard they try. (Me, for instance: I am never going to be able to play professional baseball, no matter how much I want it. I just haven't got the arms. Or the legs. Or the eyesight. Or that *thing* that make you a pro ball player.)

You're about to enter a profession (or you're already in it) where you're going to be challenged every day, where rejection – like it or not – is a way of life. That's not meant to be discouraging, or a 'downer' – it's just a way of life for a salesperson (and, for that matter, for most everyone who chooses to pursue a career that offers the potential of a high return on investment. Ask any professional dancer or actor, writer or politician, real estate agent or researcher. They can tell you *tons* about rejection.)

How do you survive that? And how, in turn, can you take what you're told – even the most difficult, hurtful rejection – and turn it into something that can make you even better at what you do?

By knowing *who* and *what* you are to begin with. By being realistic – no, more like *brutally honest* – with yourself from the outset. That way and *only* that way, will you know if the person who just said "No, and here's why ..." to you is telling you the truth or just blowing smoke. Because you already *know* the truth.

The Agonizing Reappraisal

Back about a thousand years ago, President Lyndon Johnson found himself in a terrible spot. He was running a *very* unpopular war in a country *very* far away, and he found that he had to make some *very* unpopular decisions about the future of America in the conflict. It doesn't even matter what the decisions were; he just knew that whichever direction he went, whatever decision he made … he would be unpopular with many, *many* people.

So what did he do?

He was honest. He spoke to the American people and told them that it was time for them all take a long, hard look at their place in the world – to be brutally honest with themselves, and see the world for what it was, no matter the consequences.

"It is time," he said, "for an *agonizing reappraisal.*"

Fancy words for a simple and very difficult act.

We will talk more about honesty in sales in future, chapters, but let's begin here: you need to take the time to perform a personal assessment – a specific, thorough, agonizing *reappraisal* of your own strengths and weaknesses.

This is entirely private. You're never going to show the results to anyone else, not even your closest family or friends. You're not going to add up the numbers for some misleading "final score." In fact, the whole "test" format is just a trick to get you to focus on the subject for a few all-important minutes. You can't really "pass" it or "fail" it. But like a test, you can learn a great from this assessment.

It's important, too, that you take the time *write you answers down*. Don't just skim through the questions and say, "yeah, yeah, yeah." *Think* about them. Take your time. And when you're finished, go back to the beginning and check your answers, because you're going to be looking at the document again – often – as time goes on.

So take a moment, Take a breath. And agonize.

MY SELF-ASESSMENT

Date: _____

(Each question – except for the "last one in each category" – should be answered using the standard 'sliding scale' – '1' being the worst, the poorest, the least desirable, and '10' being the highest, the best, the so-good-it-can't-be-improved. If you are like most people – and you are, face it – you will have very few if any scores of '1' of '10.' Nobody's that good (or bad).

Appearance:

____ I always wear attractive, well-fitting clothing.

____ I shave every day (or for a woman – regularly).

____ I have had my hair cut/styled in the last few days or weeks.

____ I have purchased new clothing in the last two months.

____ I use deodorant all the time.

____ I would rate my teeth as:

____ I would rate my skin as:

____ I would rate my nails as:

____ I exercise at least three times a week.

____ I have no chronic conditions, small or large.

____ I can climb a flight of stairs without becoming winded.

____ I am at or near my ideal weight.

____ I get compliments on my appearance often

The three things I need to improve the most are:

_____

_____

_____

Behavior

____ I have excellent driving habits.

____ I take good care of my car.

__ I have not had a moving violation in the last five years.

____ I pay my bills regularly.

____ I am in a reasonable amount of debt.

____ I do not drink to excess.

____ I do not use recreational drugs.

____ I do not gamble excessively.

____ I rarely lose my temper.

____ I like to tease my co-workers and family.

____ I am considered the 'life of the party' by my co-workers.

____ I am considered a "wallflower" by my co-workers.

____ I am considered a "team player" by my coworkers.

____ I go out of my way to help new employees, even though who are not co-workers.

_____ I let new employees sink or swim on their own.

_____ I tell a pretty good joke.

_____ I may not tell jokes, but I have a good sense of humor.

_____ My laugh is attractive.

_____ I do not use sex (appeal) to get what I want.

_____ I have good table manners.

The three things I need to improve/work on the most are:

_____

_____

_____

My relationships with others

_____ I always remember the birthdays of friends and family.

_____ I always pick up the tab at lunch or dinner.

_____ I am happily married or in a long-term relationship.

_____ I have a desirable number of close friends.

_____ My children like me.

_____ I take care of my pets myself.

_____ I volunteer regularly.

_____ I attend church regularly.

_____ I am always often on time.

_____ I sent thank-you notes.

___ I host a party at least once a year.

___ I donate a significant portion of my income to charity.

___ I often 'fix up' my co-workers on dates.

___ I enjoy and spread gossip.

___ I never lie.

___ I sometimes lie, but only to spare feelings.

___ I sometimes lie to get what I want.

___ I often lie to get what I want.

The three things I need to improve/work on the most are:

_____

_____

_____

My Sales Techniques

___ I often give customers cuts in prices (new customers, old customers, special occasions)

___ I send frequent e-mails or stay in touch by phone on a regular basis.

___ I am considered an 'authority' on my chosen industry

___ I often take customers to lunch, dinner, or sporting events as an incentive to buy more or keep buying

___ I intentionally overstate the good points of the products I'm selling to make a sale

___ I keep a file of the names and birthdates of customers and their family members

___ I will always try a last-round up sell.

___ I will make up deadlines, contests, or imminent price increases to close a sale.

___ I always send a follow-up or thank-you note (e-mail or snail mail) to customers after a sale, larger or small.

The three things I need to improve/work on the most are:

_____

_____

_____

Use It or Lose It

You may think that only that last section on "My Sales Techniques is really important, that the rest is just incidental. You'd be wrong.

Every aspect of your behavior and your personality that's listed above has a direct effect on your ability to sell. Because the process of 'selling' isn't *just* a matter of knowing what buttons to push or what offer to make. It's one of the oldest cliches in the business, and it happens to be right: when you're selling something – *anything,* really, any item, any service – you start and end with selling *yourself.* And that means *all* of you, from the first impression to the last after-sale *sayonara.*

So now that you've done the scoring, and gone back a second time and adjusted those scores for *complete* honesty … go back a third time. Concentrate on that last question in each section: *The three things I need to work on/improve are …*

Yeah. Do those again. And now choose the *real* goals, the ones that you think you might never be able to achieve.

This is why you'll want to keep this book close by from now on. Because once a month, on a quiet afternoon at home or in a coffee shop after work, you'll want to pull this book out and go to the next and last part of this chapter: the page that's all blank lines, split into twelve months.

Your follow-up. Your *real* scorecard.

And twelve months from now, open this book again, back up a few pages and re-take the entire Assessment. Calmly and completely observe the changes – or the lack of them – that you've achieve. And then go at it again.

We'll talk a lot about how *follow-up* is important to you as a salesperson, and that's no less true when you're following up with *yourself*. So taking that hour or so once a month and checking in, seeing how you're doing on self-improvement is even *more* important than the honesty you just offered up.

Bottom line: you want to be a successful salesperson? Good. That begins with being a good *person,* and both of those goals require steady, consistent, and sometimes painful commitment.

Welcome to the real world. You'll find it's full of challenges and risks … and if you're like me and the people I know and admire, you'll find it's worth every minute of investment.

Good luck. Keep track.

And now, on to the fun stuff ...

HOW AM I DOING?

The monthly update on your Assessment Goals

Month #1:

This is what I have and *haven't done:*

_____

_____

_____

_____

_____

_____

This is what I have to do *next:*

_____

_____

_____

HOW AM I DOING?

The monthly update on your Assessment Goals

Month #2:

This is what I have and *haven't done:*

_____

_____

_____

_____

_____

_____

This is what I have to do *next:*

_____

_____

_____

HOW AM I DOING?

The monthly update on your Assessment Goals

Month #3:

This is what I have and *haven't done:*

_____

_____

_____

_____

_____

_____

This is what I have to do *next:*

_____

_____

_____

HOW AM I DOING?

The monthly update on your Assessment Goals

Month #4:

This is what I have and *haven't done:*

_____

_____

_____

_____

_____

_____

This is what I have to do *next:*

_____

_____

_____

HOW AM I DOING?

The monthly update on your Assessment Goals

Month #5:

This is what I have and *haven't done:*

_____

_____

_____

_____

_____

_____

This is what I have to do *next:*

_____

_____

_____

HOW AM I DOING?

The monthly update on your Assessment Goals

Month #6:

This is what I have and *haven't done:*

_____

_____

_____

_____

_____

_____

This is what I have to do *next:*

_____

_____

_____

HOW AM I DOING?

The monthly update on your Assessment Goals

Month #7:

This is what I have and *haven't done:*

_____

_____

_____

_____

_____

_____

This is what I have to do *next:*

_____

_____

_____

HOW AM I DOING?

The monthly update on your Assessment Goals

Month #8:

This is what I have and *haven't done:*

_____

_____

_____

_____

_____

_____

This is what I have to do *next:*

_____

_____

_____

HOW AM I DOING?

The monthly update on your Assessment Goals

Month #9:

This is what I have and *haven't done:*

_____

_____

_____

_____

_____

_____

This is what I have to do *next:*

_____

_____

_____

HOW AM I DOING?

The monthly update on your Assessment Goals

Month #10:

This is what I have and *haven't done:*

_____

_____

_____

_____

_____

_____

This is what I have to do *next:*

_____

_____

_____

HOW AM I DOING?

The monthly update on your Assessment Goals

Month #11:

This is what I have and *haven't done:*

_____

_____

_____

_____

_____

This is what I have to do *next:*

_____

_____

_____

HOW AM I DOING?

The monthly update on your Assessment Goals

Month #12:

This is what I have and *haven't done:*

_____

_____

_____

_____

_____

_____

This is what I have to do *next:*

_____

_____

_____

CHAPTER THREE

Know What You Are Selling

Let's start with the obvious: selling a specific good or service isn't a matter of memorizing the catalog, rolling into the customer's office and slapping down the order form. Apart from actually talking to the individual – and we'll back to that in the next chapter – you actually have to know *what you're selling*.

And in fact, you're actually selling *two* things: you're selling *the thing* and you're selling *what the thing does for your customer*, or more precisely *the benefit*.

First, let's talk about …

Selling "the Thing"

If you're like most of us, you're actually selling more than one "thing." And in truth, it doesn't matter if it's a physical object or a subscription or a service. It's still a *thing* in the eyes (and mind) of the buyer – a *thing* they're about to give you money to purchase and use.

So it's absolutely vital that you understand that *thing* from top to bottom, so you can answer virtually any question that's thrown at you about it. Yes, that can frequently involve memorizing boring specifications. It can even mean talking to the people in another department (R&D, Production, Editorial, or even – God help us – *Marketing*) to get all those specifics right.

But it's more than that. You have to understand the science or sociology *behind* the product. Because there are three questions that your customer is almost certain to ask you, if not right off the bat, within the first meeting:

- What does *the thing* do?
- How does it do that?
- Does it do it better than *the thing* I'm already using (or considering)?

(Yes, we're about to approach that age-old challenge, *dealing with the competition*, but let's get in front of that first.)

What does the thing do?

In this instance, we're talking specifically about what it does: *It sucks the grit off your carpet; it keeps your feet warm in cold weather, it processes accounting information and gives you readable, accurate reports.* You'd be amazed at how often new or not-quite-successful salespeople struggle with answering this simple, fundamental question ... so don't be like them. Work it out. *Write* it out, if you have to: build those one or two sentences that say, in plain English, what *the thing* is and what it does.

You don't have to worry about fancy 'marketing' language or positions at this point; we're talking about the basics. It's almost science. Just be clear in your head: *this is what the thing does.* Do this, do it well, and you are *guaranteed* to have a cleaner, clearer 'pitch'; the people you're talking to will admire and respond to your frankness and straightforward approach, even if you don't do anything else to craft it, because you're clear on what it is you're offering.

Just remember: one sentence. Two sentences tops. This isn't the pitch. This is the *explanation.*

How does the thing do that?

Again: your new friends in R&D or Production can probably help you out here. And you don't need a new college degree to answer this question; the fact is, the person you're talking to is probably no more an expert in the science or psychology of the product than *you* are. But having at least a rudimentary understanding of the process that makes this product special will service you well: *It sucks up the grit in your carpet using electrostatic energy that virtually 'magnetizes' the grit and draws it out ... It keeps our feet warm through a combination of an electrochemical heating surface under your feet and space-age insulation ... It processes that information using a breakthrough microchip and brand new algorithms built by our own scientists.*

Yes, you'll see that competitive positioning and "unique selling propositions*" are starting to creep in here, and that's okay; frequently you'll need them explain what it is your *thing* really *does* do. But again, we're talking couple-three sentences here. Unless there is something *truly* unique about your product or service – something that really requires explanation beyond the knowledge or skill level of your buyer (e.g., *this is the first vacuum cleaner that actually FLIES!*), don't waste too much time or energy on these particular nuts and bolts. Dazzling them with diagrams and statistics isn't nearly as effective as you might think, but you *do* want to give the customer the sense that you actually know what the heck you're talking about – that you know the product and its underlying reasons for existence.

The Power of Saying "I Don't Know"

This is as good a place as any to bring this up.

There are going to be times and places – *many* of them, face it – when you will be asked a question about the technology or design of your *thing* that you just can't answer. In that eye-blinking, deer-caught-in-the-headlights moment after the question is asked, you will be tempted – *sorely* tempted – to make something up. Improvise. Dazzle them with word salad.

Resist the temptation. Just swallow your pride and say these magic words:

"You know what? I don't know … but let me find out for you."

It's usually *not* a good idea to break the mood at that moment by picking up your cell phone and calling your buddy in Manufacturing. But it *is* a good idea to actually do what you say: make a note (and make a point of *showing* your customer you're making a note), and when you have a moment after the meeting – *as soon as possible* – make that call, get that answer, it fire it off to the customer through e-mail or voice-mail.

This isn't just honest – which is a good thing all by itself. Saying "I don't know, but I'll find out" at this crucial moment is actually a *good* thing.

Because here's the secret: *the guy across the desk from you probably doesn't know either.* Yes, sometime three are buyers who will challenge you, test you to see if you actually know what you're talking about. But if you've done a reasonable amount of preparation – as we've talked about already – then you *will* be able to answer – and probably already have – any of the really important questions already. They're just pushing. Or – far more likely – they really *don't* know the answer, and they think they should, if only to explain to *their* bosses (or rivals, or co-workers in Purchasing) why they bought your *thing* instead of the other guy's *thing*.

Most important, it illustrates to your potential customer that you're a trustworthy person. That you're willing to tell the truth, even when it might not make you look so good. And at base, building that kind of trust is your Number One goal in the sales process.

Besides, it never works. Any halfway decent buyer can smell smoke, especially if it's being blown up his or her backside.

Does it do it better than the thing I'm already using (or considering)?

Ah. Welcome to the world of *competition,* of *positioning.* Trust me: you won't like it here, but it's a place you have to visit every now and then.

But really: you should recognize the terrain. You don't live in a vacuum; you live in the real world. And you make competitive decisions yourself every day: this restaurant or that one, this laundry soap or the other. Starbucks or Peet's. So there's nothing to be afraid of. And nothing to be surprised by.

Just remember: you're learning the basics of what your product or service is and how it actually does what it claims to do, you'll want to learn how it does it *differently* than the other guy's *thing.* What makes your *thing* unique? Or, in fact, does *anything* make it unique?

Keep a firm grip on your hard-earned "brutal honesty" here. Don't get caught up in your own (or your Marketing Department's) hype. If your *thing* really isn't any better in outcome than your competitors', you better know that. It just means you have to find another reason to sell (see "All Hail the Competition," in a box at the end of this chapter).

It's also very important that you realize/remember that there is *better* ... and then there's just *different*. Don't mistake the two. Even a semi-sophisticated buyer will know that you're just rearranging the deck chairs when you go that route; he or she won't give a grip about technical details they scarcely understand, but they will rapidly come to the conclusion that you're making it up as you're going along, or wasting their time with trivialities.

All too frequently, when they *do* ask this third question, they're *really* asking you about the *outcomes,* and how that matters to them, not the *processes* – unless, of course, there's some actual meat on that bone.

This brings us to the other, even more important part of Knowing What You're Selling ...

Selling the benefit of "the Thing"

There's an old line in sales and advertising I've heard a thousand times, and I hate it more every time I hear it: "It's not the steak you're selling, it's the sizzle."

That's ridiculous. Really. It *sounds* cool – very Mad Ave. – but it's nonsense. And worse, it muddies up a far more important truth.

The actual point?

When it comes to the product or service you're selling, you're not *just* selling *the thing* ... you're selling *what the thing can do for the customer.* You're selling its *benefit.*

Saying you're selling the "sizzle" is a cynical assessment of your buyers and your industry. It says that you can sell a product based entirely on the cleverness of your pitch, or its pretty design or its momentary popularity or the celebrity who's endorsing it. And that may even be true, if all you're trying to do is make *one* sale on *one* day. But if you're interested in real, long-term success, *sizzle* has nothing to do with it. The *real* cliché should be, "You're not selling *just* the steak, you're selling great taste, satisfaction, and a memory that lasts a lifetime."

In short: you're selling the *benefits of "the thing,"* pure and simple ... and when you're learning what your product or service *does* and *how* it does it, you should also build and internalize one more message: the one about the benefits. Because this is the next – and in some ways the single most important – question of all:

What does it do for me?

"Me" can mean "the company;" it can mean "the bottom line;" or it can mean – well, *me*. The person sitting right in front of you or at the other end of the phone connection. Franklin Roosevelt said "all politics is local," and it's equally true that "all sales is personal." It all amounts to the same thing: we are *all* wrapped up in our own self-interest, in finding the things that makes life easier, safer, more enjoyable. And that applies to the widgets you buy at work or the products you buy off the supermarket shelves.

So back to our three examples. After you've explained what your *thing* does and how it does it, and how it does it better, you whip out your last little gem: *It means you spend half the time you used to in cleaning that carpet ... It means you'll never have cold feet again ... I means no more expensive errors or wasted effort. You'll make more money more easily in less time.*

That's what benefits are. They're the thing(s) that *matter.*

It can take a little while to dig down and find those benefits, and you want to spend the time doing that digging. The closer you can get to basic, fundamental, human *needs,* the better off you'll be. *It will make me safer* is better than *it's the most popular. It will make me richer* is better than *it will increase productivity. It will let me spend more time with my family* is better than *It will smooth the supply chain dynamics in a significant way.*

Spend as much time as you need to discover your *thing's* real benefits. You will find great power in them ... and you'll be using them again more than once, especially when we get down to the art of The Close, which we'll discuss in detail in a later chapter.

So forget *sizzle.* Think *satisfaction.* And dig down to discover that basic benefits before you make your next meeting.

All Hail the Competition

Don't be afraid. Competitors are like … well, let's say "eyelashes." Everybody's got 'em, and sometime they can make you cry.

How can you learn about your competitors? Well, your Marketing Department or your boss may have a White Paper all ready and waiting for you, but those reports and the people behind them tend to spend a lot of time doing "competitive analyses" and measuring "market share" and such. For the most part, you can just accept the report or sit through the lecture and … let it go. All you *really* need to get from all that is the names and players, because you *will* hear them when you meet your customers, maybe on a daily basis. "Yeah, Bob from SuchandSuch, Linda from TheOtherGuy, was just in here. Great people, *great* company."

In the real world – away from marketing and 'mentors' – there are only four things you need to know about your biggest competitors, and once you know their names, you can boil it down to four bullet points:

Product
Price
Service
Salesperson

That's it. One or more of those elements are all that stand between you and a sale over the competitor. Pure and simple. And all you need to do is memorize the top four or five competitors in the market and know those four things about each of them. As in:

"CompetifTron sells the same product using the same tech, but ours is faster and more efficient. We're also a little more expensive, but our service department is rated the best in the county. And they do have the sharpest salespeople in the business."

Ask your boss or your colleagues the few questions required just to answer those four simple points: product, price, service, salespeople – and you'll know everything you need to when the competition comes up.*

So what are you waiting for? Get to work.

*The statement above is often called the "Unique Selling Proposition, or "USP" in those endless, boring books on selling and marketing. Fine. You put mascara on a mongoose, it's still a mongoose. But learning – or building, if you have to – that little nugget will come in most handy when talk about the dreaded competition rears its ugly head. So skip the fancy nomenclature and just learn it. Quick.

CHAPTER FOUR

Know Who You Are Selling

This one's easy, right? It's the man or woman across the desk from you: the buyer. Sell him or her, and you're set.

If only that were true.

Decision-makers and Influencers …

In every company – even the ones that consider themselves "entrepreneurial" – there is *always* a chain of decision-makers. There's the person you're talking to … and believe it, 99% of the time, they're a person *above* him or her and *below* him or her on the company that is equally impotant in the selling process. That's not to say you don't need to address and convince the person right in front of you – you *do* – but it would be naïve to think that this is the only person you need to be concerned with, directly or indirectly.

Everyone who's significant in this sales daisy-chain is either a *decision-maker* or an *influencer*. Generally the people up the ladder have the official "yes/no" power – they have to sign off on the expenditure, they have to approve the budget, or even if they don't officially approve it they can still stop it or delay its implementation – or worse, they can inhibit your ability to become the "regular vendor" for this product or service, requiring extensive, expensive, and time-consuming re-sells with every new order. But the people *down* the ladder – the ones the decision-makers talk to, or use to evaluate proposals, or have to get on 'their side' if there's a new product, service, or vendor in the works – have just as much (maybe more?) gravitational pull than the COO.

If you haven't already learned this small reality, learn it now: titles mean nothing. You may be talking to the Managerial Director or the Supervisor of Product Acquisition – the guy with the big corner office and the expense account – and he may have no more than an *influencer* sitting at the desk outside his office. True, you have to start somewhere, and *this guy* may be an inevitable 'meet' in the process, but it is relatively rare that your *first* contact will be your *last* contact, especially if it's an especially large sale or one that is likely to recur over time.

Sorry, but that's life in Corporate America in the twenty-first century. And it's probably been true for as long as there have been corporations. Or governments. Or kingdoms.

… and knowing the difference

So how do you tell the players without a scorecard?

It's not easy, but generally speaking you'll be able to build up the knowledge you need by doing three things:

- A little research
- A lot of paying attention
- Asking questions (but be subtle)
- Planning for more than one meeting

Doing research is far easier than it used to be, thanks to our friend and foe, the internet.

Subscribing to one of the "business intelligence" web services may work to your advantage, depending on your industry. The trade publications you get and ignore most of the time can be of help, too. But simply going to the company's web site, Googling (or Yahooing or Asking or whatevering) the company's name *and the name of the person you're going to meet* almost always yields up *some* useful information, though company websites have become a lot more 'opaque' in recent years. (There were days, not too long ago, when you could get whole employee lists and phone numbers from the web site. Those days are gone.)

At the very least, however, and in as little as half an hour, you can have a pretty good sense of how big the company is, the range of goods and services it provides, its position – or lack thereof – in the local community, and the names of at least the top players in any of the departments that might be decision-makers or influencers for you.

So as you're netsurfing, be sure to take a few notes. Make sure you get the spelling right. The return may be small, but again, there's always something to be had. And you'll be far more likely to feel and act well-prepared when you go in to that first meeting. No "So, what does your company *do,* anyway?" questions – unless, of course, you want to be done quickly and free for lunch.

Paying attention begins with the first contact – the first person who picks up the phone. Sure, this may be the receptionist, who does nothing more than stick to the script and transfer you call, but make no assumptions: get her name if you can. Keep taking those notes. And when you show up in the lobby and begin to wait for your first face-to-face appointment, you'll be able to call her by name … and almost *nobody* can do that on the first trip.

She'll remember. She'll like it. And she might even talk about it later. (Again: who are the influencers? There isn't any master list, so make no assumptions.)

Next up the line is often an administrative assistant (regardless of the actual title). In many cases, this person – usually but not always a woman, even in a world of female execs – is supremely influential … and very tough. If you think a basket of muffins or a bouquet of flowers on her birthday is going to make a good impression, you may want to think again. Not that she won't accept either one – she will, happily. But 'decorative' 'secretaries' are an artifact from the days of *Mad Men*. These twenty-first century A.A.'s are smart and hard to impress, and can smell insincerity on you like something nasty on your shoe. (They're also much more difficult to learn about prior to the face-to-face. They don't get their names in the papers; they don't get awards -- at least now outside the company).

Your best approach? Number one: *get their name* and *get it right*. Use it – though not in every single sentence, *please!* – and be sure to address them by that name in the follow-up 'thank you' notes and subsequent phone calls.

Number two, and far more important: *respect them.* These women are very frequently overworked and underpaid. The last thing in the world you want to do is waste their time, and they've seen 'your kind' a million times before. So don't try to buddy up to them, don't immediately start complimenting them, and whatever you do, *don't* flirt with them. All of that just gets in the way of doing their job, and doing the job is Job One.

So what *can* you do? Look them straight in the eye; *do* listen to what they say and respond accordingly. Don't tease them, denigrate them, or dismiss them. Try in every instance to relay the idea that *I'm here to make your life easier, not more difficult; I understand what you're going through.*

On more than one occasion, I've had accounts saved by administrative assistants who have given me a quick call, a secret e-mail or even a whisper in the lobby to let me know some crucial bit of information: the boss is in a crappy mood today, there's a big budget shake-up, he just saw Magda from CompetiTron yesterday. But without exception, these women did this *not* because I had given them gift certificates to The

Olive Garden on Easter, or had complimented their earrings on my last visit. It was because they had come to *know me* and *trust me*, and knew that I would continue to make their lives easier if I was on board. In short, they knew I *respected* them, so they returned the favor … and saved an account.

As for your first meeting with the in-your-face decision-maker … once again, make no assumptions. Almost certainly, if you've gotten this far he *is* the guy (or one of the guys) that's going to sign the purchase order, but he may very well *not* be the *only* one who signs it. Still, you might as well assume at the outset that he is. Have your conversation, make your pitch, and make your offer. And unless you've hit the bulls eye square in the center of the red circle, expect to hear, "Let me take a look at your proposal; we're seeing a couple of other people, and we'll get back to you soon."

That answer alone tells you a couple of things. "We" are seeing some others? The idea that there are other candidates in the mix should come as no surprise and is, in the long run, of no consequence. But the "we" implies that there *is* more than one person in the decision chain. It also tells you that this process is going to require additional contacts – maybe face-to-face meetings, maybe not. So now you know your work isn't quite done.

Here's where your preliminary research may come in handy. You are now ready to move to Point Three in the process …

Asking questions. Obviously you *don't* want to be blunt or even insulting: "Well, if *you* can't make the decision, who *can?* I'll talk to *them*." Not only is that a guaranteed exit strategy it's naïve: it's rare than any one person in a company (these days) has that kind of power. *Everything* is done by committee, and you should have known that going in. Now you're just trying to fill in the Points of Interest on the map. So try this instead.

"So," you say, "Would it be a good idea for me to put together a letter to Dave Jones [the head of Purchasing – whose name and rank you learned in your internet research]?"

His response to that question will give you even more information. He'll say something like "No, Dave doesn't have anything to do with this; it's just me and Mike." And you know that Mike is Mike Brown, the COO – research again. So you know (a) he's not in this alone, (b) Purchasing isn't a power center, and (c) watch out for Mike Brown.

So you keep going. "So what is it you think he's looking for most?" you ask. "Is he a price-over-performance kind of guy?" The response here may very well help you craft that letter, but even negative information will tell you just how influential he is.

If, in fact, you get the "Well, really, I just need to see a few more candidates," you will still have gathered valuable intel. You'll know he isn't sold yet, of course, but you may also know that – as much as he may like you and your products or service – he *has* to work through the company protocols of multiple vendors, or he simply has to think about it before saying yes. You can learn about the company *and* the buyer ... *if* you *pay attention.*

What you don't want to do is try and close right then and there. That's why I've listed **plan on additional meetings** as a separate step right from the outset. Whether it's an old habit, personal preference, or company policy, it is increasingly rare to make a sale – especially a big sale – in a single visit. So don't even try. *Don't* push to close at this first meeting if there's any sincere hesitation at all (and there probably will be). It will make you look impatient or even desperate.

Turn it into an opportunity instead. If you're convinced he's alone on this, ask him, "Is there anything else I can tell you that might help you out?" Keep your four "competitive points" in mind: *product, performance, service, salespeople*. If he *can* say 'yes' right now and he's *not*, chance are very strong that it's for one of these four reasons ... and some subtle questions may help you discover what it is.

But don't push. If he wants to know more about the technical specs or the process, tell him you'll send him some information. If he's clearly just going through the multi-candidate motions, be sympathetic. "What, you've got a whole week of these meetings? What fun for you?" He'll only appreciate the understanding, you're likely to get a sense of just how much longer it will before he really can make a decision ... and that will give ou a target date for your next contact, but *before* he's making that critical choice.

All in all, consider this first face-to-face as an intelligence-gathering enterprise as much as a real, live sales call. If you leave that meeting with a strong idea of the entire chain of *decision-makers* and *influencers,* then you've done your job, and you're ready to map out the rest of the successful sales process – the one that ends in *yes.*

Do perks still work?

It's an excellent question. Maybe it's a matter of age.

It's not that anyone *hates* getting free tickets to local sporting events or gift certificates to good restaurants. Who hates a muffin basket?

The question is, does it really help you make a sale? Even if you've successfully identified the entire decision-making chain, will gifts and free meals and three-martini lunches actually help? Or are they artifacts of a bygone era?

In my experience? The answer is *both*.

I've seen a distinct dividing line between those who stay with me longer and buy more because of these 'perks' and those who don't. That line seems to be "anyone born before 1950" and "anyone born after 1950," give or take a few years.

It's not that the older buyers are more corrupt or more greedy. Not at all. I've had just as many not-so-subtle offers for kick-backs and bribes from 'younger' men (and even women) than older ones. It's more a matter of habit and culture.

Older buyers think that the tickets and meals and muffins are *just the way you do business*. They don't care about them to the degree that they *need* those things. But they have come to expect them, and for that kind of buyer the absence of the perk tells them – completely incorrectly – that you're not serious about this, that you're not professional, that you're not a 'player' (though that's a term that none of the buyers "of a certain age" would ever use).

Personally, I've had more success in becoming a friend, colleague, or ally of an important customer by donating to their favorite cause, participating in their company's fund-raiser to financing a pizza day for the whole department or staff than I've ever had in getting them tickets to another game, another play, another concert (unless, of course, the concert tickets are for their teenager daughters, in which case I have done them a HUGE favor and they'll buy anything I'm selling.)

So having them in your pocket may actually be beneficial … but use them sparingly and wisely, and assume nothing.

And do a mini-agonizing reappraisal of their usefulness every year or two.

Friends, Colleagues, and Allies

I just used a trio of terms there that I believe are the real key to Knowing Who You Are Selling Too. As I've said with annoying persistence, they're not just buying your *thing,* they're buying *you* … but that begs the questions, "Who are you to them?"

You're a friend, and/or a colleague, and/or an ally. If you're lucky, you're two out of three. If you're all three, you are *in.*

A Friend is just what it says: you actually *like* the person across the table. You spend time together outside of work, your families know each other, you know what they're like outside the office. (This can be a good thing in some ways, and both painful and risky to your happiness in others. Just ask anyone who's had to say 'no' to a friend and follow it up with the horribly accurate phrase, "It's just business. It's nothing personal." Still, the workplace is where we all meet the people who become our friends, so it's not something to resist or ignore. Just know where the friendship begins and ends.

A colleague is often reserved for someone who is of a similar age and experience-level in your industry. If you're an old vet who's been around awhile, you will recognize someone just like yourself across the desk in a matter of moments. You'll find yourself quickly running through your personal list of friends, acquaintances, and organizations to see who you know and where you go in common. This is perhaps the most powerful, if not the most productive, relationship you can hope for. This colleague *knows* you and well as your business. He or she (in my experience, especially *she*) is a terrific source of new referrals, important industry news and speculation, and even sales. Colleagues are honest and reliable; the more you have the better. But they are not, ironically enough, a guaranteed source of orders. After all, you are now part of their 'inner circle', just as they are for you. *Not* buying from you isn't an act of war; you're going to know each other and work together in the future, and none of the more common manipulations will work at all with a colleague – you won't use them anyway, why risk the valuable long-term relationship? Still – *colleagues* are good, even great. Cultivate them at every opportunity.

Allies are the best of the lot when it comes to sales. You don't have to like each other; there doesn't need to be an deep *personal* relationship or any shared history. There just needs to be a deep and sincere mutual understanding that *you make me look good.* Yes, it's situational – it may change over time, and not always for the better. But in fact you can talk frankly and honestly with an ally, you can give them bad news as well as good, and you can rely on repeat business and referrals from them because *it's in THEIR best interest to do so.*

This goes beyond just having the best price or best tech support. This is about the perfect marriage between *supply* and *demand,* with a healthy dose of *enlightened self-interest* thrown in for good measure and though it requires a certain amount of care and feeding, it can work well for everyone.

Allies are what your every one of your regular customers need to be. And all the research, attention, inquiry, and follow-up you've been doing is the best way to make those alliances.

Becoming the resource they really need

There's one other level – one that's more strategic than tactical, one with long-term benefits but a fair amount of short-term effort. But if you're committed to staying in your own particular territory, in your own particular industry, for the foreseeable future, consider the advantages of becoming a *resource*.

This is essentially selling without selling. This is about becoming an authority who offers advice and insight about your chosen business *without a sales pitch attached.* Not even down the road somewhere.

- You can publish an e-newsletter on the field
- You can do speeches at the local trade association or business group.
- You can speak at trade shows.
- You can write articles for trade publications.
- You can build a small circle of close friends – buyers and fellow sales-people that you share job referrals and personal information about birthdays, births and deaths.

In sort, you can become a valuable resource to a wide range of influential people, without an specific or immediate goal beyond simply sharing information.

Why bother? Because in the long run, *sales will come to you without you asking.*

Seriously. It works.

- You'll get tips from Person #1 about a change in personnel at Company B, which is provides you with a great opportunity nobody knew about.

- Person #2 will listen to your speech at Conference D, and invite you to come and talk to his people about the same subject. Shortly thereafter, you'll walk out with an order.

- Person #3, somebody you've never even *heard* of, calls you one day because Person #1 (remember him?) said you were "the guy" when it came to answering questions about such-and-such. The call leads to a lunch, the lunch leads to an intro, and suddenly you've got the hot new exec at the newest company in town signing the purchase order.

This isn't a short-term selling proposition. It's difficult to measure. But if the field you're in is something you actually enjoy, if it means something to you, consider putting in the extra effort to become that *resource*.

I will pay off. It has paid off for me over and over.

Common Ground Making Connections

There are whole lot of books on selling – whole contact management systems – based on the idea that *the more connections you make with your client base, the better the sales.*

I don't agree.

I can send out birthday cards 'til I'm blue in the face, and join all the 'right' tennis clubs and golf tournaments. I can even choose what church to go to based on my client list. I can pretend to be Sherlock Holmes when I make m on-site visits, learn all I can about the customer's family, reel off the names of children and birthdates of people I've never even met (and never will) …

But I don't believe – not for an instant – that it will make me one dollar more, or at least not enough to make all that worthwhile …

... unless it's sincere.

When my kids were babies, and I discovered that a particular customer had kids the same age, we would talk about our kids. Endlessly. And I'm sure I took home larger, more frequent orders from parents like me because we felt a connection there. Nothing wrong with that.

When I met a customer whose parents were struggling with arthritis the way my Mom did, we shared a lot. And again, I probably got more and bigger orders because of it.

But these are connections that happened in the natural order of *getting to know my customers*. They cannot be manufactured. They cannot be *forced*. And you can (and should) build your client base on something *other* than sincere connections, because the sincere ones don't happen all that often. (See **Allies**.)

Making connections with customer is a good and productive idea. In fact, they're a very rewarding part of doing business. But if you really want to make them solid, don't make them up. Reach out and discover them.

Almost all companies (and decision-makers) have made commitments to one or more local charities, whether the subject is breast cancer, Alzheimer's or the YWCA. It's no more difficult than scanning the bulletin board in the coffee room to figure out where their corporate and personal interests lie.

Contributing to those groups is good. Contributing through the company's or the individual's specific fund-raiser is even better. And actually showing up, helping out, getting involved it best of all – *but only if it's important to you* (for some reason other than a commission check).

Folks appreciate *sincere* effort, but it's terribly important that you realize how vital the *sincere* part is. They will happily accept your money, as long as it's not counterfeit. But they won't accept (or believe in) your involvement unless *that* is sincere, too.

The return on those investments extends far beyond your sales quota for the month. Just don't get confused about what matters most ... and what's nothing more than manipulation.

Sex

Let's talk about sex. Just for a moment.

I'm sick to death – have been for a generation – of hearing from disgruntled male salespeople about Saidie or Sarah or Cynthia who "just uses sex to get the sale." Like it was a magic potion you could pour into some buyers' *caffe latte* and walk out with an order.

So let's agree on two things:

- Sex may open the door, but it doesn't close the sale. At least not more than once.
- Women aren't alone in this, and never have been.

Let's face it: there are even statistically valid studies now that show *pretty people get treated better.* What a surprise. People who didn't figure that out by the second grade just weren't paying attention.

But attractive women *and men* only get one advantage over the rest of us: they get about another thirty seconds up front. People (including but not limited to potential buyers) will *automatically* pay attention to a handsome man or a great-looking woman for a few seconds, even minutes, longer than they'll pay attention to you ore me. That's true. Their physical attributes give them that. But if they don't follow that up with brains, sincerity, good humor, honesty, and a product worth buying (to mention just a few of the essentials), the prettiest eyes or most beautiful hair in three counties will not get them the order. And if they infatuated fool on the other side of the desk *does* do that – and it's amazing how rarely that happens – he won't be doing it for long.

Because the people up and down the line – who are paying the bills or trying to use that under-performing or over-priced product or service – didn't have the benefit of viewing those long legs and smelling that intoxicating perfume, and they'll be even less impressed by the guy who's relaying on physical attributes alone to get the order won't be getting any *re*-orders, and won't be having a chair at the big boy's stable for long.

That's what I believe.

And remember, men have been using this same tactic for as long as there have been two genders. Whether it's physical attractiveness, personal charm, or just a nice set of specs, handsome men are just as likely to use it to open that door as any woman with a great figure.

So enough with the bellyaching. Sadie or Susan or Cynthia got that order because *she's better at sales than you are*. It's up to you to change that.

CHAPTER FIVE

Know How You Are Selling

It's a crazy world, isn't it?

It was not so long ago that all a salesman needed was an order book, a working car, and shoes with sturdy soles. Maybe access to a desk with a phone on it.

Not so these days. Now selling is a multi-media event, and not just because it's cool. It's *essential*.

Let's take a couple of minutes to reiterate the Old Truths, and then admit there are plenty of new opportunities that modern tech and society are offering up.

The face-to-face meeting still carries the greatest selling power of all. It is *very* hard to simply ignore a human sitting right in front of you. You can't hang up on him the way you can a phone. It's even hard to *interrupt* a real, live person in a real, live room; most people won't even try. Like Shakespeare said, "It is the mightiest of the mighty; it becomes the throned monarch better than his crown." And all other forms of communication do nothing more than seek to duplicate the "live" experience. It's that powerful.

No matter how easy or intriguing other media become, don't abandon the face-to-face meeting. Don't even avoid it. And don't underestimate it, either. For all the fancy camera, microphones, and high-speed internet connections available to us, the very best of them in concert can only emulate a fraction of the power that in-the-room, in-the-eye selling can offer.

The smartphone has become a truly remarkable device. Many decades ago, when The Phone Company was trying to encourage long-distance calls (can you imagine that?), they said talking on the phone was "the next best thing to being there." That may still be true, but the 'telephonic experience' has changed entirely since those days, and mostly for the better. Voice-mail alone has changed our lives (young'uns today claim to not even *recognize* the busy signal.) And it allows salespeople to stay in touch like never before, making short, unplanned, and essential contacts about appointments and customer service from anywhere at any time. Of course, the *disadvantage* is the exact same thing: you are reachable on the phone anywhere, at any time. It can make it hard to have a life. A few rules of thumb:

Don't pitch, or even *chat*, on the phone. Convey the information you need to and get the heck off. Remember that the telephone is *not a sales tool* in and of itself. It is a *communications tool*, an adjunct, meant to facilitate sales in some other medium (face-to-face, e-mail, internet).

Do *not* call customers outside of business hours unless there is some specific emergency where they have previously instructed you to do so. Nothing can do more damage faster than an outside-of-hours call that the client does *not* see as essential.

No texting, photos, or multimedia messages. As much fun as they might be, none of those are appropriate for business communication, not even on the coolest smartphone in town.

THEY don't have to be available 24/7, but YOU do. And that truly is the downside. If you're in any kind of business that involves shipping, deliveries, equipment breakdown, or customer service of any kind – and who isn't? – you are now *expected* to be available to your customer base at any time, twenty-four hours a day. Get used to it.

E-mails may be the single greatest boon to sales craft in the last 100 years – and I'm including telephones. As I said, the phones are a nice little helper, but you can't really *sell* on the phone (unless you're one of the poor wretches we piteously call "telemarketers," and the less said about them the better). But e-mails? E-mails do everything that snail-mail of the past did, but *better* (with one exception – see below). You can convey information, make pitches and proposals, offer special deals, and carry on a detailed conversation that is *not* bound by the restrictions of time itself. And now, with e-mail linked to smartphones, they can reach clients when they're not in front of the computer at all. I can't help it: I love e-mail. I depend on it. But even e-mail calls for a few simple rules:

> **Keep the e-mails short and sweet.** If you have a long proposal or even a long explanation or answer to give, do it in an attachment, as a more formal document. The e-mail itself should be no more than one screen deep.

> **Think carefully about the "subject" header.** Don't just make it "For John" or "About our meeting". Make it more self-

explanatory; encapsulate the message that follows. "Thanks for the meeting; see you Tuesday" is much better than just "Thanks."

Don't make them too pretty. It's easy to get carried away with graphics, emoticons, logos, embedded images, animations – all the bells and whistler. But remember, these are *business* e-mails. Keep them plain and simple.

Always add a digital signature. Virtually every e-mail management system like Microsoft's Outlook or Apple's Alexa includes the ability to have your "signature" included on every e-mail. You decide what goes in the signature, like your name, your title, your company name and your phone number. Be sure you've done this. Use it all the time. You never want a customer or potential customer to be searching for your phone number or address, and you don't want to waste your own time typing it over and over.

E-mail newsletters

Let's take one second to talk about one of the must *under*-used forms of sale craft: the e-mail newsletter.

This is not the place where you actually make sales. That's still a face-to-face process for people like us, and probably always will be. But you can use e-mail to supplement those expensive sales calls, and stay in contact with your entire customer base on a far more regular schedule that face-time allows, using even the most basic and available e-tech.

Check our applications like Icontact or Constant Contact. Look at other simple and inexpensive or even free programs that are widely available. All of them do the same basic thing: they allow you to send an attractive and easy-to-produce newsletter to your entire client base in a matter of minutes.

And the fact is, you can send these newsletters to your contact as often as you like, and they will *welcome* them. One every three days – every *day*, even. Truly. As long as you follow one unbreakable rule:

Only e-mail a newsletter when you have something important to tell them.

No cutesie holiday greeting. No recipes. No cartoons you thought were hilarious. And no straight, vague, go-go promo language they've heard a thousand times before.

Give them *real information* about changes in the industry. Make *real offers* for discounts or sales on items this particular group might actually *use*. Talk about breakthrough technologies or great new products or even economic issues that affect you all.

If you can do that – if you can say something *real* and *important* in every edition of your newsletter – you can reach out and touch your customer base as often as you like, and they will thank you for it. They'll reply with e-mails of their own; they'll mention them at your next sales call. You may even sell a few things based on the offers or "online only" sales you try.

On the other hand, if you waste their time with empty dreck *even once* … prepare for the consequences. Lots of resentment, lots of angry e-mail, and plenty of addresses that are suddenly blocked.

E-mail newsletters are a powerful tool. They can transform your business at a basic level. And they can also kill it if you're not careful.

Consider yourself warned.

Is there a role for social media?

We define "social media" as all those quick, fast "groupy" things like Facebook, Twitter, Tumblr, and whatever's hot this week (hey, remember MySpace? Neither do I.) At times these seem the exclusive realm of teenagers or younger, but that – for good or ill – is changing.

Take a serious look at your market. Unless you have a very large and rapidly changing product line, and even then one where you need to get short bursts of information on what's available *right now*, most of the social media probably aren't for you (they're certainly not for me).

Facebook may be the one exception. There is a growing effort to make Facebook an inevitable part of your life with features like the Social Reader, that can redefine the internet 'space' for you. But here, too, you have to have a reasonable belief that many – *most* – of your potential or current customers are already active on Facebook in some professional, grown-up way. If not, you'll be forced to try to get them to 'join up', which is tough and time-consuming. If they *are* on Facebook, they may still be using it primarily as a way to talk to family and non-work friends, and they won't appreciate or respond to a 'business' presence in their 'private' sphere.

This may change in the future, but it hasn't yet. Keep an eye on this continuing social phenomenon, but don't count on any worthwhile business application in the near future – no matter how much fun it looks like, or how much time your teens are wasting with it.

The iPad and other tablets

Did I say that e-mail was the greatest sales tool of the last fifty years?

I lied.

This is the greatest sales tool of the last fifty years: the iPad and its tablet brothers and sisters.

When I think of all the years I spent hauling around samples cases as heavy as lead, or fumbling with slides and overlays ... it is to laugh.

The iPad and all similar tablets have given us the ability to do *incredible* face-to-face presentations, quite literally at the press (or tap) of a button. You don't have to be a genius at PowerPoint or similar applications – not anymore. What you can't put together (or have Marketing put together for you) you can get from a local college kid for next to nothing, and the return on that investment will be immediate and *huge*. Animations, point-by-point presentations, photographs, even video, all embedded in the pitch that you used to have to struggle to provide even in the most 'prepared' environment.

If you haven't made the jump to tablets, you're overdue, and you won't regret the changeover for an instant. If you haven't started using it to its full potential, this is the *one* time I'd suggest taking a class or a seminar and learn the full potential of your tablet as soon as possible.

The only caution – and it's a real one – is to avoid the temptation to get *too* fancy. You may remember a similar time – if you're old enough – when PowerPoint presentations first came into being. It was *so* easy to get carried away – to do twenty slides when five would do, to put everything into glittering rotating bullet points that would chase each other across then screen and then blink in rhythm to the *1812 overture*. Don't do that this time. Stay in control of the tool, or it *will* take control of you.

Other than that … go get 'em!

The power of the written word

Finally, let's double back to the beginning – to the second-oldest form of sales on the planet: the actual written word.

And I don't mean *typed*. I mean *written*.

Hand-written communications have always been a powerful medium, even when there were few alternatives. Today, what with voice and video and IM and all, actually putting pen to paper has become even more unusual and more high-impact.

Don't overdo it, of course. It would be … odd, somehow. But do *not* leave the thank-you card or the "quick note to a friend" out of your arsenal.

An unusually shaped envelope with a hand-written address will almost *certainly* be opened by the legendary "gatekeeper," and if the (short!) message you've written is sincere, it will just as certainly wind up in front of your customer.

I'm not suggesting you use it as follow-up for every face-to-face visit … but for a big order, after an important referral, or when you become aware of a major event in the customer's life – a birth, a death, a wedding a graduation – don't overlook its power and importance.

And practice your penmanship, please. It's practically a lost art!

So how are you selling?

Very well, thank you … by using every variation of instantaneous communication that the world has to offer: the internet, e-mail, smartphones, social media, podcasts, YouTube channels… Now just wait 'til holograms come along

CHAPTER SIX

Know Where and When to Sell

Aren't you embarrassed by the stereotypical "salesman" character who will try to sell whatever it is they're selling just about *anywhere*? In the line at Starbucks, at a wedding reception, during the coffee hour after church. Real estate agents seem to get that bad rap more often than anyone else, but it doesn't seem to matter what it is that poor desperate soul is pitching. I've seen everyone from produce wholesalers to "afterlife planners" – what we used to call *morticians* – plying their wares in the most inappropriate places.

Don't be one of those people. It doesn't work anyway; the quality or longevity of clients you acquire by jawboning at every social gathering in sight just aren't worth the effort.

That doesn't mean you shouldn't *network* at every opportunity. Talk to people. Tell them what you do. Learn names, collect business cards, follow up all the time … but please, for Pete's sake, *don't sell all the time*.

You make us all look bad.

When and where to sell

On the other hand, things have loosened up considerably in the last ten years. I blame it on Starbucks and the iPad, but the fact is there *are* more acceptable venues than they're used to be … and a few fairly obvious ones that have gone wanting in recent years as well.

The Office

The office remains the #1 place to do you business, and should: it's where decisions get made, and it's at least *possible* that you can get even the coldest call to make that decision right then and there, ten minute into your first meeting.

My own opinion is that this is the *only* place where that first, all-important *yes* actually occurs – the more casual alternative are great for follow-up or initial introductions or keeping warm leads from turning stone-cold, but the real business of the day requires a presence in the office.

Make it your default. *Keep* it your default. *Assume* you will be meeting your new customer (or an old one you're re-upping) at his or her place of business, and plan – as always – to get there a few minutes early and dress appropriately. For all the flexibility of the Modern Age, don't devaluate the power of the workplace. Quite the contrary: *own* it. *Dominate* it. Because fewer and fewer of your rivals are taking it seriously, and that is to their detriment.

The coffee shop

When future historians write of our time, they will undoubtedly call is the Starbucks Era. How could you *not*? There's one on almost every corner. Their number in any given community seems to outnumber churches and hospitals combines, and there are *always* customers. I can't recall ever walking into a Starbucks (or any of their rival chains, for that matter) and seeing it empty.

The prevalence of coffee shops like Starbucks is both a blessing and a curse. It allows easy and convenient access to a 'neutral territory' for customers old, new, and potential, and it's true: it's much easier to get a 'yes' from a reluctant or over-busy customer if you're only asking them to walk down the street to Starbucks rather than clear an hour for a sales call.

But everything that makes Starbucks a good thing makes it a bad thing, too. It *is* always busy, so it's always noisy. Even finding a seat can be hard. In most coffee shops, tables are far too close together, so serious or extended conversations can be difficult at best. And forget about talking money or details of the deal. Anything even approaching proprietary or sensitive information simply isn't going to change hands in a public place, and for all is fake 'intimacy,' Starbucks is *still* a public place.

So use it – but use it appropriately. First meetings. Follow-ups. Casual contacts. Choose one that's near to the customer's home turf, and have a nearby alternative in mind if it's just too crowded or too noisy. And *always* try to angle back to that all-important "money phrase:" *Let's take this to the office …*

Business groups

As I've mentioned elsewhere, you can find new leads and even make half a pitch in some unexpected places … and one of them is local, community-based business groups. It may seem counter-intuitive, especially if your industry is not consumer-based. Still, it turns that these groups are the essence of *networking*. People know people. Friends, neighbors, family members. And if they're already part of this group, each member is self-selected to *help*.

So try it. Invest a little time. Talk to folks, and see if, in turn, *you* can offer some unexpected leads. You may very well see that investment returned to you tenfold. And you might even have a decent meal.

Conference seminars

Trade shows and conferences got a bad rap in previous decades, when – let's face it – many of them were simply excuses get away from the office (and frequently the family) and party down with near-strangers.

The harsher economic environment of the 2000's has changed that. In fact, it threatened to kill the conference/convention business entirely for a while. But now they've come back – if not stronger than ever, at least with a new and more realistic purpose.

Many of the surviving conferences or conventions, especially the ones staged by the larger trade organizations in your industry, really *do* attract the best speakers and the most influential minds. At the very least, you'll find yourself attending presentations, roundtables, and workshops where you can learn some fascinating and even useful information about your industry. But you can also turn the table here and potentially make some sales.

Months in advance of the next big conference – at least six months, maybe more – contact the organizers and offer to stage a seminar of your own. Choose a subject you actually know something about; consider inviting a few of your best and most articulate customers along as speakers as well (especially if the conference and/or those clients are relatively local, or can fly in for the day cheaply).

This is *not* a thinly veiled sales pitch. This is legitimate information that could be of interest to colleagues. The thing is, potential customers will be there too, and even those colleagues can be rich sources of referrals: to clients that are out of their area but in yours, to customers who need something you offer that the colleague doesn't have in his or her product line, or as strategic partners where even larger and more ambitious project can be made real.

Of course this can happen just by wandering around, working your contacts, or haunting the exhibition hall. But it is far *more* likely if you make yourself noticeable … and many of these conferences are hungry for good content. Consider it. Come up with a concept that *is* worthwhile. Invest the time and see what happens. You may be surprised.

Speeches and self-made seminars

The power of the seminar is not limited to far-off conferences. The local branch of your trade association is, most likely, even *more* hungry for guest speakers that your regional or national conferences. There may even be opportunities to set up seminars or workshops of your own with their help. Consider it either a reiteration of your "national" work or a test platform, so you can hone your topic and presentation before you take it up a notch.

Many of your colleagues and rivals attend trade shows and trade organization meetings as well, but – most of them, anyway – in a lackadaisical, "I have nothing better to do, I guess" kind of way. My suggestion: go all in or go home. And there may, in fact, be some gold hiding there, if you do a bit of digging … and put yourself out there.

CHAPTER SEVEN

Know How to Close

This is not going to be a long or complicated chapter.

There are whole lot of books, DVD, entire DVD *series*, dedicated to the Art of the Close …

… and quite frankly, I think most of them are just .. **Ridiculous**! A waste of time.

I've seen them all. I've read far too many of them. You've got your Half-Nelson Close, your Critical Confrontation, your Block and Tackle, your … never mind. If you've browsed the "Sales" sections of your local Barnes and Noble, you've seen what I'm talking about. If you haven't, save the trip.

I have never been a believer in the 'psychological' approach to sales – the idea that your customers (or all human beings, for that matter) are just little computer made of meat, and if you say the right things, use the right phrases, push the right psychological buttons, you can *compel* them to say yes to whatever you want.

If that were true – if the writers those books really *could* do that – they'd be kings of the world, and we'd be under their spells.

Last time I checked, we aren't.

Sure, it's possible to manipulate or pressure a buyer – especially a new one – into giving you an order. But in the long term – even the mid-term – that's counterproductive.

Using pressure or manipulation to close a deal is like kissing your best friend's girl. It may feel good at first, but you hate yourself afterward … and it never goes anywhere good.

In fact, you're not (or shouldn't be) looking to make just *one sale,* and using sneaky or intimidating tactics to get that *one sale* is a waste of time. You're looking for *allies,* you're looking for multiple sales over a long period of time, and that kind of relationship *cannot* begin with bullying or manipulation.

The real closing process

There's no mystery to it, no mumbo-jumbo. It comes in three parts:

- Identifying the obstacles to "yes"

- Overcoming those obstacles

  (*Rinse and Repeat*)

- Asking for the order

It's as simple as that.

Every potential buyer has concerns. Some of them are legitimate: the price is higher than they want to pay, they're concerned about making a large commitment, their boss *insists* that she talk to at least five vendors. Some of them are not: they had a bad lunch, they never buy from women, they really don't have any intention of buying; they're just checking prices.

So how do you identify the obstacles? Okay, go with me here. It's a challenge. It's tough. It's risky!

Ask.

You have a good product – you know that. You've made a good presentation. But you can see it: the buyer is still on the fence.

You may have your suspicions. You may recognize that look, that body language. But as difficult as it may be, there is *absolutely no downside* in going straight at it:

You ask, "So what's keeping you from making the decision right now?"

And then … you *pay attention.* Listen to what the buyer is saying and *not* saying. Engage your b.s. detector and turn it up to 11.

My own belief is that *most* people, when asked directly, will tell you a *version* of the truth. They'll leave out parts and polish it up a bit, but you *will* get important information. And because you're likely to get only part of the truth at first, you may have to repeat Steps One and Two a few times before you get to the all-important Step Three.

If it's price, you see what you can do. Discounts *do* work, even one-time cuts, but only use them when it's clear that – really, no kidding, that's the issue, and it's not just a matter of 'scoring.'

If it's a technical concern – that this isn't precisely the product or service they may need – then you return to a mutual process of education: *what do you need? What can I offer?* Sure, it will be a temptation to shoehorn your product line to meet their 'needs,' but resist it. Chances are there's some other creative alternative to lying (or even fudging) … though ultimately, you may have to walk away, make a valid referral, and know that you've made a good impression that will pay off in the long run. (No. Seriously. It will.)

If it's bureaucratic – that there are other people that have to see the proposal, sign off on the deal – then try to meet with them *right then,* before you leave the building. If that's physically impossible, spend just as much energy trying to get a specific day-and-time appointment in the *very* near future. And if *that's* impossible, do your best to *not* walk away without the name and e-mail of the higher-ups, and some idea of what it is you can do to grease the wheels.

Specifics are the key, in each of these cases and the other five thousand I haven't mentioned. Try not to settle for vague "I don't knows," or "maybe later." *Yes,* after all is the *natural* response to your presentation. What's stopping them?

You don't get if you don't ask

Which brings us to the last point – the simplest and most neglected point of all.

Ask for the order.

You would be amazed – *amazed* – at the number of new salespeople who come to me and say, "I just can't get Buyer A or Decision-maker B to say *yes*. I've covered all the bases, overcome all the obstacles, bought them a wonderful lunch, and *still* …"

"So," I said, "How did you ask for the order?"

They blink at me like I'm started speaking Latin. "Um .. I said *You can see this is a good idea* or *So you agree that this is a good investment for your company? Or I understand your bottom line: you want to make more money. We want to help.*"

"But," I say, "Did you ask for the order?"

"What?"

"Did you pull out the order book [or contract or whatever] and say, "So how about fifty units at $12.50 a unit? I can have them here by Thursday.""

"Uh ... no. They ... they didn't look ready ... they didn't seem receptive. I didn't get a positive answer to my last ...""

"So you didn't ask."

"Um ...""

"They never said *no,* because you never *asked.*"

"Um ...""

And that's the end of that conversation.

All too often, it's really no more complicated than that. You need to look your potential buyer in the eye and make an offer: a simple, one-sentence reiteration of the order that can only end in *yes* or *no.*

And then you stop talking – *STOP TALKING* – until they give you that one-syllable response.

I've known more than one new salesperson who were brilliant talkers, charming people, knowledgeable about business and the industry they had chosen. But ultimately they were bad – or at least mediocre – salespeople, only because *they couldn't bring themselves to ask.*

It takes some grit to ask for kiss or the clout, right there right now. And to a degree all the pitching, schmoozing, and set-up is a way to *avoid* getting to this moment.

But you have to do it. You have to embrace the darkness, Luke, and *ask.* Because the ultimate truth in this business is exactly that:

You don't get if you don't ask.

And if you *do* – if you get used to, even *comfortable,* with that edge-of-the-cliff moment, without backing away or avoiding it entirely – you really *will* sell more. It really *will* be easier. And then – just like the title says – *all* the keys to success in sales are within your reach.

CHAPTER EIGHT

Practice Makes Perfect

I said it at the beginning and I'll repeat it now: being a successful salesperson isn't a matter of pushing a few motivational buttons, learning a few tricks of the trade, and applying the Half-Nelson Close. It's more a way of life than a set of instructions.

On my best days, I like to think of it as similar to the life of a professional athlete or a dancer. You *live* sales, really. You think about it; you train for it, you change your off-duty life to accommodate it as often as not.

And just like the life of an athlete, being a good salesperson required constant practice, even when you're *really* good at it. The renowned business philosopher John R. Covey calls it *sharpening the saw*, and I've always appreciated that term. Getting good and staying that way, staying *sharp*, is a bit like the repetitive, focused act of sharpening a saw.

But that doesn't mean it has to be onerous or boring.

I tend not to read books or articles about *selling*. They fall into two categories for me: things I already know and things I don't care about. But I do love to *talk* about selling, and the physical and mental challenges it presents.

So here are a few ways I sharpen the saw. I suggest you consider similar approaches, or make up your own.

Books and programs on selling. Stay away from seminars, DVDs, or books on selling (other than this one, of course!). They're a high and mighty waste of wind.

Join and actually *participate* in your local trade association. It's almost a foregone conclusion that your particular industry – manufacturing, publishing, information technology, heavy machinery, agriculture, etc. etc. – has a regional trade association. The sad fact is most of them are dying in the face of harsh economic times, a lack of money, and a lack of involvement. So change that: get involved. If you really do love the work you do, this will prove it: you'll find people – both competitors and non-competitiors – who are just as enthusiastic about your line of work as you are, and you'll learn a *ton* about the changes in the industry, what's coming next, and – of course – how to sell. The networking opportunities are obvious and rich, of course, but the good it will do for your motivation is immeasurable.

Get on the board of a non-profit or two, and focus on fund-raising. Here's better soul-work that can help you with your selling skills, too. There *have* to be a dozen different non-profits within walking distance that could use a smart salesperson on their board. Choose a cause – one that has a real personal connection to you, whether it's related to health issues, social issues, young people, or the elderly – and get to work. Focus on the all-important issue of fund-raising. It will give you a chance to put your selling skills to work *and* see how they work an in entirely different environment. And of of course you'll be doing something for the good of society at the same time. How is this a bad idea?

Join and *participate in* a local business group *not* affiliated with your industry. Most people join these groups of local businesspeople – groups that meet for breakfast or lunch once a month, exchange stories, listen to speakers – and then drift away after a few months. They look on them only as networking opportunities, and when they don't live up to expectations, or when they feel they've tapped all the contacts they're likely to find, they quit. But that's not the idea here. The idea is to make a few friends *and colleagues* in your area, and see what you all have in common... Because selling widgets, it turns out, is not all that different from hawking macramé or moving pork parts. You may very well pick up some insight as well as some great stories, and you'll certainly feel energized by the right mix of people. And there could actually be gold in them hills. My brother-in-law was a compressor salesman – big, ugly, sheet steel *compressors* – and he swore to me for years that he consistently made sales in the most unexpected places from contacts he made in that local, random business group. (Guess you just never know who's going toned a compressor).

Teach. You want to know the best way to sharpen your skills? Try teaching them to someone else. Writing this book – even as a months-long exercise in dictation – has been a tremendously valuable tool for *me,* making me look at all my own preconceptions and discovering truths and patterns I really hadn't seen before. You can do the same thing, but volunteer to teach a class on sales at the local City College or extension program. This is part of being that *valued resource* we talked about earlier: learning more about yourself and your work by selling without selling. And once again, you may accidentally do something good for your community by training up after *really good* salespeople. 'Cause Lord knows there are never enough to go around …

ABOUT THE AUTHOR

Thank you for buying and reading this book. It has been an unexpected pleasure and a real revelation to me, from the day I began to this very moment, when I'm finishing up.

For the moment. Because you never know *what* else I might come up with.

In the meantime, happy selling!